THE GIVEN

BOOKS BY DAPHNE MARLATT

The Given (2008)

This Tremor Love Is (2000)

Readings from the Labyrinth (collected essays, 1998)

Taken (novel, 1996)

Two Women in a Birth (with Betsy Warland) (1994)

Ghost Works (1993)

Salvage (1991)

Double Negative (with Betsy Warland) (1988)

Ana Historic (novel, 1988)

Touch to my Tongue (1984)

How Hug a Stone (1983)

Net Work: Selected Writing (edited by Fred Wah) (1980)

What Matters: Writing 1968–70 (1980)

Zócalo (1977)

Steveston (1974, 1984, 2000), with photographs by Robert Minden

Vancouver Poems (1972)

leaf leaf/s (1969)

Frames of a Story (1968)

To Susie,
with affection and
thanks,
Daphne

THE GIVEN

| DAPHNE MARLATT |

McCLELLAND & STEWART

LIBRARY AND ARCHIVES CANADA CATALOGUING IN PUBLICATION

Marlatt, Daphne, 1942–
The given / Daphne Marlatt.

Poem.
ISBN 978-0-7710-5458-7

1. Mothers and daughters – Poetry. I. Title.

PS8576.A74G59 2008   c811'.54   C2007-906590-2

We acknowledge the financial support of the Government of Canada through the Book Publishing Industry Development Program and that of the Government of Ontario through the Ontario Media Development Corporation's Ontario Book Initiative. We further acknowledge the support of the Canada Council for the Arts and the Ontario Arts Council for our publishing program.

Typeset in Scala by M&S, Toronto
Printed and bound in Canada

This book is printed on acid-free paper that is 100% recycled, ancient-forest friendly (100% post-consumer recycled).

McClelland & Stewart Ltd.
75 Sherbourne Street
Toronto, Ontario
M5A 2P9
www.mcclelland.com

1 2 3 4 5   12 11 10 09 08

For Bridget

For Bridget

The whole thing: just trying to be at home. That's the plot.

ROBIN BLASER

We also change like the weather.

PEMA CHÖDRÖN

Contents

SEVEN GLASS BOWLS

| *overture* |

you remember – what is it you remember?

the feel of home, that moment of coming into your body, its familiar ache and shift, its little cough of consciousness resuming (Monday claims). i'm awake. i can't quite see your face assume its usual definition. your shoulder rises like a hill i climb getting out on my side of the bed to pad to the sunroom, lift the blind on a spectral world. one early dog racing across the park, its breath steaming up through pallid light, though it isn't light, not yet. still in bed, you turn to rise like some revenant, asking what time is it?

in the still of the day we bring something to burn. the smells of home, not roasted barley flour but tea, tea and toast. these small ceremonies ribbon through the days we share. and share, continuous, with what is gone.

it was July, that radiant kind of morning when all of outside shines in, calling the body out to play, light pristine, re-arisen, chickadee's two-note shrill euphoric, *here / i'm here* – this *joyant* pouring in with sun across a kitchen nook amist with memory smoke, his breakfast cigarette, my usual struggle with a five-year-old, eat your cereal, you can't go out until you eat. while all three of us know, between sips of this and that, only two blocks away the waves are lapping tenderly at sand, at soon-to-be bare feet, a thrill of seaweed under the gulls' dip and shriek.

how it was, that morning of liquid flight when my father's call came: i can't wake her up, his voice like a child's, crushed, lost. i've tried, she won't wake up.

and birds, in the corner of an eye as i stared unfocused at their skywriting: flap flap, soar. their Sanskrit.

why does the eye slide off? the mind refuse anything more than grabbing at keys, making quick arrangements, then tearing through the parkway across the bridge along the Upper Levels, thinking glorious glorious morning, everyone driving their usual cavalcade of must-do's and if only's, thinking how can this be? this sudden gap.

gape. a wound that is love and not love.

you can't do that, she told me over the phone when we'd come back to the city and i wanted to paint what would be the baby's room. you can't paint when you're pregnant. that limiting fear i bridled at. it's latex, Mom. we painted together in a memory loop from my childhood, water instead of turps, a splotch of robin's egg blue on the soft sag of her cheek, her perfection at cleaning brushes. paint moons at the roots of our nails, and her latest conspiracy theory about her doctor, her dentist.

A pleasant glow of sentiment was shed by a light rosily shaded and suffused.

that too. its pleated shade, its fluted glass stem a little tippy, casting a glow to read by. satin quilt pulled up to her chin, hands holding the well-used public library smell of plastic covering a queen's unbent head, the bloody intrigue of courtiers and kings, while all the while steam rose from the rose-patterned teacup beside her, twisted and thinned to nothing in the pinkpearl glow.

rapid overlay, one place-time on another, as if we're actually in the movement between, memory cascading its light-drenched moments and then suddenly that single jet of recognition, parallel perhaps, that allows us to see, para-doxically, this place we're in the midst of . . .

incredible. conflicting with explanation.

underlay, as if
her body under the
lay of the city under
lies it

to feel at home in just that particular light before haze moves in – moments only – brightens Spode blue mountains dusted white today. Crown leaning its dazzle over the blue shoulder of Grouse. against their steady presence the restless filigree of leafless birch. waver, tremble. still getting used to this particular sense of history as missed story, shadowing place.

clop clop (oh) clock. the Grand Canyon Suite she'd iron to, that syncopated beat filling the house when i came in from school, dumping books on the camphorwood chest (*you're late – what have you been doing?*), fresh linen air of line-dried sheets seared now in the heat of the press (*did you eat your apple or give it away?*). not even turning her head, burn mark on the inner flesh of her forearm . . .

on, little donkey . . .

her loopy scrawled hand – *Just keep me – Guide and love me Lord – Just for today* – inside the cover of *The Plain Man's Book of Prayers*. one day at a time.

we bring what there is to burn in the still of the morning, the trace of a smell for those who can only eat what is burnt. candle flame and water.

exit signs flashed by me, exit from the rapid urge to get there, reach the end (of what?). cars rushed by me in their focused race to the ferry or to work, digital numbers rolling up on dashboards. time, that net, tightens in around us (just to know / i don't want to know), numbered exits adding up.

where there's a will there's a way. one of the maxims she passed on from English children's books meant to curb bad temper and boredom. i still remember the child who had to gather every scrap she'd torn up in a pique. the girl who had to carefully unpick her own imperfect stitching. shadowy figures i tried not to pass on in turn. those mauve goads dyed deep in her, and farther back, mauve half-circles under my grandmother's eyes.

. . . the incessant swing of our despair between this love and its
body . . .

what to do with the body?

picnics like flares in the contained monotony of August days home at loose ends bickering. broken by her packing us all in the car for Deep Cove. the shrieking plunge. salt hair smell of the dog's stubborn haunch. goose pimples, chiggers, tar. salt-thick fingers waving bread and cheese around in a kind of wordless inner hum, mmm, lost tomato half-moons dropped on sand. immersed in what held us: wind off the cove, mountains leaning down. and far far off, the unplumbed shimmering stretch of Indian Arm –

time to go.

or coming home,

that other kind of distance. the long stare in her eye across the dinner table when she looked at one of us as if we were a stranger sitting there. long distance eating with us alone.

as in *the case of destination after a vb. of motion*: going home

this gearing down for the turn and rise up the steep ascent of their driveway – like the "old house," the steep ascent of that last bit of road, and then the turn onto the hump of driveway. a part of me still shifts into that gear, undying adolescent, simply she who relives the whirlwind of maternal fury after the finesse of easing in, killing the engine with just enough momentum to make that glide, lights dimmed, weight of the blue and white Pontiac (all metal then) letting me coast so as not to wake her on the other side, the head of her bed against the carport wall and she a famously light sleeper.

i come to a stop and stare at the stone wall of their retirement garden. Dad's green hose for watering his roses, the "magic path" my son "discovered," sense of tiptoe-trespass

down through overhanging bushes – not exactly over-
grown, but something hidden, bushing out.

oh gioia, that cry she did the ironing to, a joy that would be
cancelled, she knew, by the demands of the story. opera /
work. the work of fate.

behind it, another very tall house not in Hyde Park Gate,
with its tea table, its servants and guests, its *tyrant father* –
theatre for family scenes.

so how does it feel to be back? friends ask. and you,
"back" after a long hiatus, some twenty-eight years
spent elsewhere, in England, almost all of your adult
life, you hesitate. not a backtrack, this return to a city
you were glad to leave once, city that changes its face
every few years. you temporize, well, this is new to me,
this neighbourhood, it was never part of my inner map.
and you leave it at that: a house you mostly love, a
tough little eastside neighbourhood you're beginning to

trust. community, that is. with a colon and a space after.

It was time, the passage of time: they eat, the children leave for school, the husband goes away, they telephone, there are the two or three small chores, they clear the table, they wash the dishes, the dishes are put away, and then presto . . . there's emptiness . . .

homing in.

we've had a couple of scam artists, you say when i return with the dog from our walk. someone trying our windows on for size, as you jiggle the screen in its frame trying to get it to fit back in. it won't, you say, perhaps it never did. what happened? two guys dressed in orange safety vests with a yellow X. claimed they were here to wash all our windows. when they picked up the garden hose you realized they'd come with no equipment, so you called Ros. no, she hadn't hired them, though they said they'd done her windows. called Pat, same result. three angry women on the path confronting two guys – not a squeegee between them, you said.

hour of the sugar refinery's horn. like some forlorn heifer bawling along the waterfront.

home is where you hang your hat, his grey fedora with the buckram band's precise and flattened bow. Dad's home, someone sings out, noticing the dog's rush to the door. the hat that would hang on a hook above his grey raincoat draped formally from a hanger and, below that, his black umbrella neatly furled in a corner of the hall. *Dad's home* the call for supper. traffic fumes, pipe smoke, tired echoes of business talk peel off him with the hat, the damp folds of raincoat reeking of wet gabardine and stale air from the neighbour's car he's commuted in – all those hours for a mere *pittance*, she says, piercing the sausages in a sputter of fat. Annie, it's your job to mash the potatoes. as his six o'clock shadow bends to kiss us.

If you go down to the woods today / You'd better go in disguise . . .

we performed it around the dining table for her, making grotesque eating motions with our paws, dancing with heavy legs in burlesque mimicry. collapsed in laughter and got up again to whirl in the ecstatic return of the high notes, *For ev'ry Bear that ever there was . . .*

she stood in the kitchen doorway twisting a tea towel in her hands, laughing at us.

or stared out the window at the fog bank hiding a lost city, a dripping fir –

or both. both.

home and the closeness of the beloved. *The place of one's dwelling and nurturing, with its associations.*

in the stillness of morning, we set out seven glass bowls with a tea-light in the middle – two waters, a flower, incense, flame, perfume, food, music. pour water through

inner turbulence. watch it brim luminous in each trans-
parent dish. watch it through our muddied implicatedness.

overdosed on despair.

when i came in through the door of her bedroom and saw
her curled away – her body curled in itself, like a child's.
and like a child's, the body in abandon –

birch-waver, pine-sway. animated talk of struck glass.
rhythmic gusts bending the length of trunks away from
our neighbour's porch.

a gust, a new one, bends them violently again, again, and
back to still.

furor scribendi. rapid, with frantic signage, pine jostle green
behind. and always the ecstatic tinkle, mad, of glass –

Oh, gioia, that cry. *Oh, gioia*, as if the word itself would open what the iron couldn't under her hand levelling creases, nosing into the folds of boxer shorts, *A quell'amor ch'è palpito*, into the pleats at shirt's cuff-edge, pressing, *Oh, gioia*, under the collar, *Follie! Delirio* . . . a kind of sob.

what to do with the body?

(we didn't know.)

But if you ask lots of women what they do, women from low-cost housing and all that and even in the bourgeoisie, what they do in the afternoons, they say that's the problem; if there's boredom, that's where it is, during those hours. This hole in the afternoon . . .

the streaks birds make, in the corner of an eye, in a blue, blue heaven that can't be January.

home, you say, excited, this is the closest to what it means to me, and holding it up, you read in that clear, cool, slightly accented voice of yours. . . . *if by home one means not four walls and a roof, with a fire and a chair before it, but the place of one's earliest affection, where that handful of men and women may be found who alone in all the world know a little of your wants, your habits, the affairs that come nearest your heart, and who care for them.*

so where is home for you? i probe.

England of course.

the *earliest?*

i know, i know. i was twenty-four when i arrived there. but it *was* the site of my earliest affection.

the letter slips out of an envelope with its stamp torn off (pillaged for somebody's album, mine perhaps). soft paper cream-coloured and stained. addressed to my father, his initials and last name *Esq.* c/o an uncle in West Vancouver. postmarked Ilfracombe, 10 Sep 1951. details on crackling onionskin, she in transit still with three children, buying winter clothes (their first), night terrors, ear infections. what most preoccupies her is the shape that home might take:

– if you see a 4 bedroomed one – a garden not too big – the
house, light, airy & attractive – not too far from the shops – or
school – (if there is a school bus – better still) – then I suggest
you take it – if you are pretty sure it will meet with my
approval. after all – look how attractive we made Camville. but
i do want a bright cheerful house – & what i think attractive,
you do – as we usually see things in the same light.

accidentally closing the door of the car with a slam that
sounds brittle in the huge quiet i'm aware of as soon as i
step into it, i walk around the house. the top half of their
kitchen door stands open. he's heard the slam and comes
to meet me, face stricken, eyes raw and red. standing
there in his faded Viyella shirt, the father i have never
seen crying.

he holds my hand, thank you for coming, he whispers. a
gentle habit, remarkably gratuitous. of course i'd come, i
whisper back. no one else to hear.

the cat cries insistently. cries, perched on our bedroom
ledge, impossible, he says, to get down without leaping
into the warm air of the living room one whole storey

below. the cat dramatizes abandonment fear. still lost in his story of being confined to a cage for six long months, eating rabbit pellets for lack of kibble, lying with his nose against his litterbox, dreaming of home in a crocheted hammock (some SPCA volunteer had at least made that).

who alone in all the world know a little of your wants . . .

when you go to the post office, you leave with your Gore-Tex hood down over your head, mail clutched next to the harnessed cat in your arms, dog straining at the leash for the car ride that breaks the monotony of an indoor day.

think it over –

is it ever?

blue mountains very blue today. blue mountains every day.

she arrived with her portable Singer in its brown wooden case, its black machine-body kept well oiled, its golden curlicues we adored. she came prepared to make clothes, sew curtains, mend sheets.

It is cheering to know you think you can buy a house – how about the financial aspect? I'd feel happier if I thought we could go into one & stay put – not a rented one just for a few months. I'd want to put curtains (!) up – & have it as nice as possible – & then the curtains wouldn't fit elsewhere etc.

that delicate phrase, *the financial aspect* – his language, his jurisdiction. whatever was necessary she was prepared to meet, but what she longed for was "extra," "extravagant." doll after doll she dressed for church fairs, an extravaganza of lime-coloured organdy, or mauve, lace trim with delicate stitches, petal-strewn hats on tiny heads. the kind of hats she'd once worn to colonial church bazaars that were fashion parties. and her gowns? the Chinese-tailored evening gowns she'd danced in, worn to dinner parties in the tropics, on the ship, expected to wear in Canada – they stayed in a trunk. ooh'd and aah'd over by us, her only audience, trailed on the floor, fought over, they lapsed into worn accoutrements of childhood fantasy.

i come downstairs and find the cat asleep in a patch of sun, head on one outstretched foreleg on your family's old hamadan, its colours aglow like illuminated letters all around him. so still the house in sunpour, the cat detached while dogs race each other across the street in a green gusto. if all this is a sign, what does it say? one seme, one phoneme even?

cut down in her – well, almost-prime. long over the hill, she'd counter, her particular hill being forty.

lying in bed on her side, face a shade darker against the white pillowcase, one hand all we could see, the rest of her under a dusty rose blanket, patchily worn now, she'd bought in England, one for each daughter's bed twenty-four years before.

description. this writing around . . .

what was all of a piece – old bacon, wool blanket, mothball smells we walked into each time, faded Chanel N° 5 & the peppery scent of nasturtiums, always nasturtiums in the celadon horseshoe bowl, the goodnight hug she turned from, twisting the smocked neck of her nightie – the deeply familiar smell of her hair, her skin – Nivea,

and this: outrageous birdjoy all around, cheep-chirping, whistles, flirting. sun flooding the garden like a celestial bath.

her body impossibly there and not there. dumb. its fine hair she always complained of. sparse lashes folded against her cheek, all that was left from what had fallen out, she claimed, when she'd applied some patent thickener long ago:

released from her story.

the wild temptation to shake her and shout "wake up! wake up, Mom!" name she hated.

"you don't *say* mom," she would rhyme it with pom, pompom, pommy, "so why spell it that way?" but "mum" is so *English* we said, as if English were a dirty word. besides, "mum" is for anyone on a bus, in a shop – we knew that much from our months in England – it doesn't really mean Mom. the capital claim.

now i remember mum's the word.

1953

| act one |

only she, to begin with, she which means about – and so begins the long pulling of a thread from the trammel that underlies all this, the way any of us are tangled in the past. she with her little shoes and small hat, clopping down the road with a full purse like any good donkey (lipstick and comb, compact with mirror, cologne-spattered hanky, crumpled Avon calendar with its birthday record – flower of the month, stone of the month – bobby pins at bottom half buried in old powder folds, and of course the vinyl wallet with its well-used compartments tearing apart at the seams . . .)

but she wasn't walking, she was driving, a humped black Pontiac with Silver Streak Indian head on its bonnet, that era, heading home but braking to a stop in front of Burdett's because she'd forgotten tomato sauce and at least they'd have that on their shelves, dearer than the superette of course, still it meant the children wouldn't complain, so Canadian – whoever heard of tomato sauce, all right, *ketchup,* on fish and chips? frozen last resort after a late afternoon because the doctor she'd had to take one of them to, which meant taking all three, was late as usual and they'd had to wait a good forty minutes in that horror of a waiting room, airless and stuffed with women's magazines, the women themselves preoccupied with keeping their kids well behaved, the endless when, Mummy? when? oh the endless lie of it, just a few minutes more darling, long minutes to skim, against her better judgment and half-heartedly, pages full of advertisements, full of advice, *KEEP YOUR HUBBY HAPPY* ("hubby"? such awful slang), *greet him with a smile when he comes home from a hard day's work,* as if this wasn't work, this endless waiting (what right had he, that cod-faced doctor, to keep children in suspense like that), all the while listening to the sullen kicking at the chair leg beside her, now STOP it, for the hundredth time!

to sit here in birch tendril flurry, light morning breeze. at
home in the signs of a hot day – sniffing a trace of incense
from next door, sniffing for durian a few blocks away.
traces body-memory will rise to greet. facing birch waver
outside my window, leaves opaque in their height-of-
summer green, slightly sticky. flurry of leaves the flurry
of sparrow wings. some days seem miraculous, this being
in the midst of it all, this *being* at all, now that i'm the age
she was when she died.

Dummer dummer Reitersmann,
der mich nicht verstehen kann!

Lehár. Bizet. Verdi. foreign languages cascading through
the house, always to the rise and fall of ebullience, pathos,
melodic repeats.

not that her taste was popular in a city where sewers were
more to the point than opera.

this knot of the 50s – undone by a love that wells up for, as if from, the city on occasion, by surprise. as if the insistent views that keep us separate fade to thin air's embrace my heart lurches in, widening out to apparitional mountains in the haze, the close-up glittery smile of False Creek, its towers, its tugs, its 1930s bridge with glass flambeaux above the sea's old smell of bilge, of used-up sand. gull cackle. rim shriek.

Dearest Mother and Father – We arrived safely last Sunday in Vancouver. Charles met us at the station and here we are – at the very Western edge of Canada – which I can say is a very large country indeed – although we only saw it from the windows of a train. The trip across seemed interminable – Annie managed to achieve a black eye by falling against the folding table in our cramped compartment – the usual highjinks! Still we are all here – under one roof and in one piece.

and then i'm there: halfway up Grouse Mountain on that block, rainy firs dripping staccato time on a peak roof. black steel trunks on bricks in the basement lying like tombs with P&O steamship labels on them, wartime letters folded inside with cello packets of mothballs. upstairs, peanut butter and grape jelly the newest snack (*all right but don't you dare touch that knob with your sticky fingers*), we lie on the floor, three sets of ears tuned to woven speaker fabric fronting the console before us, three sets of eyes focused on its tiny amber navel as if to conjure what our ears anticipate, the opening chords of *Mystery Theatre*, its scary elsewhere. while the house settles down around us, not Canadian, but almost.

Dearest Mother – Thank you for yours. We are more or less settled, which gives me a chance to write a decent letter. The house is (well, what can I say?) *typically Canadian I suppose – heated by burning sawdust, if you can imagine – Charles finds this appropriate since he is working for a lumber firm! The rooms are on the small side – such a shame! The wardrobes we shipped from Malaya won't fit anywhere but in the cellar. But there is a sweet little Church of England – known as Anglican here – just a few doors away & a few shops on the corner of Lonsdale – rather like a High Street. On the other hand, one absolutely has to have a car – because of the distances. Fortunately the girls can walk to their school – which has the rather poetic name of "North Star" – a bit quaint don't you think? But then we are living halfway up a mountain & almost in the wilds!*

surrounded by bridges, backed up against mountains. inching forward in long commuter lines to the Lions Gate toll booths.

and no, she says half-turning her head from the front seat, we *don't* have time to stop for ice cream on the other side.

the child was busy counting them present in her book of days under <u>Wednesday</u>. *<u>Ash Wednesday</u>. Daddy feeling very ill didn't go to office. L. has sore ear. Daddy is in bed, so's Mummy. Mummy has a septic throat. Mo. & I the only ones who are well.*

Splendid, he declared of the mountains, writing home to England. Particularly on a clear day when we drive back from the city over a rather fine suspension bridge.

late afternoon refrain: time to tidy up! Daddy will soon be home. (home + home = 2.)

you're the oldest. I need to know I can count on you.

Twin mountains they are, lifting their twin peaks above the fairest city in all Canada. . . . so Pauline, beginning to tell the story of "The Two Sisters" – a name "absolutely unknown to thousands of Palefaces who look upon 'The Lions' daily." now i have a name for what we are. now i know the secret name and story of those mountains to tell my two sisters.

adding up the family: 5 toothbrushes. 2 teacups + 3 glasses of milk – set them out. 4 skirts + 1 pair of trousers. for a while that child recorded everything in 5's. plus a few extras, friends, those natural transgressors of thresholds.

<u>Saturday</u>. *Children were not supposed to play here today but Sheila came, and we ran out of chores so we played.*

or stood above the heat register, flannel nighties belling out, sudden sweet rush down there which has no name. teasing, jostling, "my turn, my turn!" crossing my legs just to feel – (no words) – slow treacle fire running through me.

– there's no accounting for –

. . . the absolute need of an alternative route into Vancouver with our two railways running up the narrow Fraser Canyon, as 600,000 people could very easily be cut off from the rest of Canada.

that glorious violin! – what had he heard? she'd been irritated at the rapture in his voice when all she heard were the hurrying chords, dark, piling up on each other. now, iron hook of the wood stove's lid in one hand, slab of firewood in the other, she's staring into the flamey smoulder while the same Tchaikovsky then as now fills the air. his revolver had been upstairs while they sat in the lounge – as if there were all the time in the world, as if he wouldn't be setting off for the mainland in the morning. all those rubber estates, whose accounts he regularly went to check, infiltrated by Communist guerrillas in the trees. a well-aimed shot from the trees would have meant the end of everything. what would I have done with three small children? well, she sets the lid firmly in place, here we are. and, anyway, I've never really liked those wretched symphonies.

and not in public.

near St. James (looks like a bastion not a church, she said, but then I suppose it has to look like that here) where the North Van ferry used to dock, we rolled from the car deck onto streets thick with foghorn sound. she told us to keep our windows up, not because of the rain but because of the men staggering off the curb (for heaven's sake, he's just asking to be hit!) in the neon glow of pub and diner. she drove straight towards the ruddy glow of that giant W, its bright aisles, sale items ringed by pushy women, its ping of cash registers. wove her way deftly from one crowded aisle to the next as we tagged behind (where's Lucy? I told you to hold her hand!), picked up this and that, assessed it, measured it against us. as we trailed out at last with our

parcels to gaze at the wonder of Christmas windows, a
blind man who sat on a camp stool shook his tin of pencils
at us. here, she said, giving us each a nickel to drop in his
worn cap she told us not to touch.

what is allowed and what is not.

writing in splotchy ink. *School Girl's Diary*, pocket size,
its cloth covers opening on a photo spread of women
hurdlers, intent, volitional, leaping over barriers. list
appended, *Careers for Girls. acting. banking. domestic science.*
hairdressing. librarianship. needlework and embroidery.
nursing. secretaryship.

her métier: the perfect dress and the search for its afford-
able version.

filling in the days. _Saturday_. _picked raspberries in the garden, did the washing up, helped Mummy peg up the laundry. Sunday. Carol was allowed to come + we had a dolls birthday party._

while writing in the red scribbler hidden on the bookshelf inside a copy of the _Girl's Own Annual_: Elizabeth was going back to sunset school but she was also going back to a queer mystery.

when i said Daddy's got his head under the bonnet they laughed at me. they said it's not a bonnet it's a hood.

my chickadee, whether we say bonnet or they say hood, it amounts to the same thing. they're both hats after all.

Red Backers. Bad Hats. at night they spoke of them in quiet voices.

Every Canadian should own his own home if he so desires. The strength of any province or nation stems from happy, comfortable homes and well-ordered families.

Dearest Mother – We have had a round of measles – The girls seem to catch everything going around their school. Father should be proud of all my home nursing – the girls are recovering nicely, no nasty complications, and Doctor G. was very pleased. But the measles are only half of it – the people on one side of us have become most unpleasant. They want to cut down all our beautiful trees – and to top things off, they want us to foot the bill!

MacLean's Method of Writing. scratching along the dotted line with a straight nib. blots and lots of spilt inkwells. turning the book to get the right, the Canadian, slant on it all. getting it right.

out of the cereal box come Mark Trail cards. Cheryl Black keeping the lamp lit as Mark traps, follows spoor, explains bush lore. lying on my stomach on the living-room carpet, face in the Sunday comics, i want to be freckle-faced Scotty learning how to survive in the bush (not the bluebell woods or the cuckoo woods but the bush) under Mark's patient eye.

"The Ghost is in the corridor!"

or was. datuk kong. shrines to them all over the island. ghost tales of how they inhabit a particular place would surface occasionally at dinner parties as he poured the wine. his uproarious laugh at what was inexplicable, un-accounted for. back there.

running a finger over the cover, its doe-soft leather with a painted Indian head and the name hand-burnt in capital letters below: E. PAULINE JOHNSON. as if skin might absorb the words inside. Sagalie Tyee, fire-flower, tillicum and Trafalgar Square. new words, and old words she thought she knew, put together strangely.

stop dilly-dallying! it's your own fault if you're late. you know the rule – you can't leave the table until you finish breakfast. you don't know how lucky you are. there are countries where children don't have a scrap to eat, let alone a school to go to!

but, Mummy, you hated school, you said so.

I didn't hate school. I hated the headmistress, but that's beside the point. everyone should be able to go to school – it's just that I was there on my own for holidays too. you should count your blessings. you have a home to come back to.

figuring out which words count.

no longer was it God Save the King. all at once in once-upon-a-time made real in a golden chariot, Princess Elizabeth, slender, grave, one of the two little princesses, came to Westminster Abbey, sat on the throne and in jewel-studded crown and ermine-trimmed robe ascended our schoolroom walls, appeared on all our coins and bills, *by the Grace of God, Queen of this Realm and all her other Realms and Territories.*

driving along Marine Drive, we could see the silver spires of the Catholic church gleaming on the reserve. but that was there. we never turned down there.

Advertising helped make "The Little Woman" what she is today . . . an expert buyer.

there she is, stylish hat and flared shortie, slender heels, black seams running straight up her calves, examining the label on a cottage cheese container.

Dummer dummer Reitersmann . . . humming as she plaits my hair, forgetting to tell me not to fidget. *Dummer dummer* . . . twisting the elastic. *Hopalop und hopalo* . . .

what are you singing?

you've heard it often enough.

but what does it mean?

dumb, dumb Riderman. she's teasing him because he doesn't understand her feelings. dumb Riderman, ride on – that's what she's saying. but of course that isn't what she really means.

sailing imagination away in folded "silver paper" from chocolate bars. playing "sardines" with our fear on rainy afternoons, the lights doused. prompting our words with charades. devising costumes for "plays" we concocted on the back lawn for her solitary applause.

three little maids from school – *first of all the three of us, Joan and Dorothy and me. oh those Xmas hols, Bombay miles away and foreign as far as they were concerned – not the nearest thing to home I had. it was Joan's mother who under-stood. dear old Gilbert and Sullivan, the Christmas panto, those theatre nights – I drank it all in. never dreaming that one day I'd be ironing clothes for three of my own on a mountain in Canada. life is peculiar.*

there was Lumberman's Arch. its felled-tree look, his stories of giant stumps he'd seen up the coast, her *of course* they'd glorify loggers here! Margo squeals at a crawling thing with pincers. earwig, he says, it crawls under your hair and into your ear like this . . . we squeal for his grin.

you don't remember the millipedes in Penang, he asks, with all their tiny feet?

and the kerengghas, and the chichaks. pushing the picnic bag aside, she settles back on the rug with her head on his lap. yes, she sighs, gazing up at the cedars that ring the clearing, this would be perfect if it weren't for our neighbours.

better the Grays than guerrillas, he points out.

Spring Rites Presaged
Afternoon Whist Party   putting your best foot forward
Stork Stories   matching high heels and gloves

North 575. black receiver and a party line.

it's Mrs. Gray (in a whisper) and she's talking about *us*.

(sudden slap)

hang up at once! no child of mine is going to be a spy!

weight in stone. other mothers measured in pounds.

running late, past Carol's house down the empty road. everyone's gone, already lining up at the outside stairs as the bell rings. wait, wait at the crosswalk for a slow bus to rumble by. what does he care, the driver with his bored look, what does he care about school and detentions? wish i could fly, wish my too-big rubbers would just lift up, unbuttoned coat balloon above the pavement, arms outstretched, higher, over gardens and roofs, gull curve and soar in endless sky –

those can't be robins, they're much too big and dull-coloured. such clumsy things! why on earth would anyone call them robins?

not naughts and crosses, not hugs and kisses (click of chalk on blackboard all through recess). three X's in a row and that triumphant crow, "tic-tac-toe!" i know how to do it. meanie! she grins back, heart-shaped face with freckles, Donna the girl from Prince George who is newer than me. we walk home together up the same street.

Granville bridge riveting guns sweet music to Vancouver ears

this is where I smell it, that deep harbour smell. the same and not the same. no sampans here. no Butterworth ferry. kerosene maybe, the same oily water dripping off hawsers, maybe the same freighters. no jackfruit or durian, no smelly chickens in rattan baskets and heaven knows what else. we're better off here, for the sake of the girls. still, Marine Drive and Capilano – I wonder whether Charles smells it here too.

you look a perfect angel! she said as the freshly ironed surplice floated down onto my shoulders.

walking up the aisle behind the golden Cross, one of the
Angelic hosts we were singing about, rounding my mouth
on the "o" as Mr. MacLaren required. trying to look the
part, except my collar itched and i couldn't scratch because
i was holding the hymn book with both hands like every-
one else. angels don't scratch. nor do angels wobble as the
choir walks ever so slowly up the aisle. Danny's carrying
the Cross high up in the air where God dwells in His
perfect power. Danny who called me *Anny-fanny*. Danny i'd
punched the other day.

**May God help the Christians of Canada rise to the challenge
and put a Godly layman in every riding.**

Marezy doats and dozy doats
and liddul lamzy tivy.

who is Mairzy, Mummy? who is she doting on?

well listen to the words, she laughs. a kiddly tivy too –
wouldn't you?

water with no time but its own running in ditches down the mountainside, running in tiny rivulets a stick makes in the mud drawn away from where it wells in the wet joy of detour. back-eddy. flow. watching how water breaks through haphazard mats of sticks and leaves that act like little dams. damn it, her father had said, standing on the chair, the light bulb not screwing in. dams won't hold, nothing holds water's insistent spill downhill. water doesn't give a dam the time of day.

Kla-how-ya, Tillicum. the only rule governing acceptance as a member of the Tillicum Club is that members are asked to live up to our motto "We're all friends together."

Donna and her sister sleep in bunk beds, one above the other, and they can talk for as long as they like after lights out. bunk beds would be fun. but we have sawdust bins that Donna likes, rolling down the hills even if we get all itchy after and have to pull all those bits out of our sweaters. she says they're sweaters, not jumpers.

I'm yours. Valentine's heart with an arrow through it. heart-shaped candies with messages scrawled across. *Be mine* disappearing sugarsweet on your tongue.

I don't see eye to eye with any of them. calling themselves The Ladies' Auxiliary – ladies? hypocrites, if you ask me. making a show of being so devoted, then turning around and stabbing someone in the back. and all those petty arguments about who's in charge of the altar cloths, who's supposed to do the flowers. that old battleaxe is the worst of the bunch. and then she turns all smarmy smiles when the Vicar walks in, yes Reverend this, Reverend that. butter wouldn't melt in her mouth.

HARD HATS AND HOT RIVETS

look, Mummy, that's Donna's dad in the newspaper photo, that's him high up on the bridge they're building over town. isn't he brave?

Dear Dorothy, how are you faring in Delhi with your Planned Parenthood? – I do hope you have had no more of those awful threats. The Mau-Mau news from Kenya is simply dreadful – Life here seems rather quiet by comparison – but we are thankful to be in such a safe country for the girls' sake. Charles is working long hours and commuting back and forth to the city which takes its toll (ah, she'll miss that, not knowing the bridge) *– but he likes the firm, thank goodness. Our girls are becoming quite Canadian, you would be amused! Do think about a visit.*

going over town
across the bridge across
the water to where
the tall buildings the lights
where he goes each day
where the world
ricochets

I'll never get the smell of bleach off these hands. such ugly chapped things, hands of a charwoman, that's what they are. and to think I used to go for manicures in Georgetown once a month. what's the point of dressing up for the Office Party with hands like these?

Kinettes will see to it that those attending the Kinsmen Carnival will be able to enjoy a quiet cup of tea.

the readers we got at school were meant to be covered in flat book-cover papers they handed out, showing us how to fold the corners neatly to keep them under wraps. how to print the subject with dark pencils, put our name and grade below.

as the months went by, we drew squiggly borders or cats or eyes depending on what appealed. slid notes inside. scribbled and erased initials. altered stains to doodles.

in June we tore the covers off and handed back our books, surprised at how anonymous and new they looked. how suddenly not ours.

OUT OF THE BLUE

| *intermezzo* |

Good Luck Tea from Harrogate, clay mug fashioned by West Coast hands. pinch of green leaves in a tea-darkened bamboo sieve, its broken handle propped by a spoon sinking under the hot pour of water. winds and bamboos, a rattan chair. gaps and continuity. watching it steep, i wonder will it help me pull all this together? *good luck!* (the sardonic refrain of adolescence.)

home gaps, gapes, like the gape of her blouse our eyes avoided. going downhill.

coming home (was it?) coming to her (body), their house, full of her taste. satin brocade cushions, mushroom colour, plumped in place. we'd sat on them for years. lemon polish under-smell of the house. in the kitchen sink, last night's bone china cup, familiar, a blur of faded crimson where her lips had sucked. English tea towel limp and slightly grubby. in the bathroom, light-brown hair tangled in her brush. sense of trespass staring at what had been part of her. these things that belonged to her, not things apart but part of her.

The old troubles, the things she had known from the beginning, the general shadow that lay over the family life and closed punctually in whenever the sun began to shine . . .

hitting home.

Time and Distance on the corner outside the once-synagogue later turned boys' club then condos. in the dark its old dome, lit from below, floats at the end of the alley like some spaceship . . . *a woman kneels, waiting, with a child. A path behind her leads away, over the horizon. Points on the curve, a piece of an arc, hide ghostly male figures* . . . emigration history, not Jewish in this instance but Chinese. families broken by the head tax. palimpsest of removals. chips of broken colour in cement. mosaic.

Something that was not touched, that sang far away down inside the gloom, . . .

fee-bee, fee-bee, the bird books translate it. or an English friend, *yoo-hoo.* the vowels all wrong. *you here? ye who?* spring's piercing call to bliss, all *ye here* . . .

and there, out of the blue,

in that peculiar mid-morning hush of the suburbs, houses shut, people gone to their various destinations. let sleeping dogs lie, she warned us. the dogs themselves sun-drowsed, content.

the body incontrovertible. does not lie.

residual. burned futon and sheet, dumped in the alley in front of our garbage cans. who dragged it for how long down the alley's gravel? and from where? pale green as in purloined hospital sheet – deliberately set on fire? some boarding house smoker's accident? to wince or not at the charred rim, the skin of someone's passage.

I had been to big cities before, but I had never seen one with such a war zone.

and roses, roses frosted onto birthday cakes, sparkling with
fake dew-diamonds on anniversary cards. organza petals
nodding from a doll's hat. yellow roses, pink roses. *for a
blue lady.*

·what to do with the body?

*. . . the longing for some fairy godmother who will arrive
at the reader's door and put her to sleep. When she awakens,
her bathroom will be full of exactly the· right skincare
products . . .*

despite shed skins of condoms, limp underfoot, despite a
worn pair of boots, one still standing askew, the other
bereft up the slope, morning rises fresh, scented with
balsam from the poplars that line the schoolyard fence.
morning means greeting solitary others. the sweatsuit,
sun-visored jogger, professionally intent, whose face on
her third? fourth? lap illuminates with "hello." the woman
who runs the corner grocery store performs her chi gong

next to its *OPEN/ Dairyland/ Your Fresh Ideas* sign. the trim
man who jogs in spats, face with the serene look of a Ming
scholar floating above light fists.

I am NOT your skivvie.

summer's here, i say, and the bodies are on display again.
the girls, the nubile, self-conscious bodies of girls. we're
passing The Drive's urban circus of stares, ruffled hips and
bare midriffs, bodacious tank tops, lean spaghetti straps
sipping cappuccino or beer. yes, you add, the large ones
and small ones, the good-looking ones and the not so good-
looking ones. i glance at you but your mirrorized shades
reveal nothing about the particular shade of your smile as
we pass by – grandmas driving the Drive.

gulls wheel and cry above the dumpsters, wheel and cry.
swoop – that lunge of desire. where does the perceiving
body begin and end?

*Leftover, stale food that no one else wants, waiting in the cold
for an hour to eat, then waiting another half hour for preach-
ers to tell us what sinners we are . . .*

stretched flat on a mossy roof, a black cat lifts its head
only to Cantonese. while, below, the retired man, portly,
pacing infinitely slow with Beau, decrepit bear of a Beau-
voir who flops and refuses to get up, waits, with infinite
patience, one hand leashed, shakes out a cigarette,
remarks on the weather, waits. crows cawing Crow in the
horse chestnut trees.

but what is it you miss?

friends mainly, London a bit – it's a much more interesting
city. and the countryside. there's nothing like that here.

so what is home then? (persisting.) is it always what we
leave behind?

my exit from her body years ago . . . connect. connect the dots. mother-body demands the daughter remember.

like burglars whispering as she lay behind us under the blanket, curled into herself as if asleep. curled up and gone. Margo and i rummage through her drawers for something, some explanation beyond the empty bottle of sleeping pills. a note, a last word to make sense of this void.

Time and distance are how we measure separation.
(in the body of the mother-text)

city's a memory-scrawl. neon allure, marquee names in capitals, The Oyster Bar. mannequin window gestures across the street, everything larger then, cinematic. Foncie's Street Photos. city lights in a daughter's leaving eyes. the Capitol, the Colonial. *Fire in the Hold* gone cold. the contrary whirr of re-, re-, re- in rebel, re-moved.

in the curtained silence of her bedroom, I turn to Margo. we should call Lucy.

yes we should. but she's so far away she won't be able to get here in time.

in time? we look at each other, stunned. it's too late, too soon, too late already. now there is only the waiting for them, whoever they are, to take her body away.

A number of persons, concepts, or things, regarded collectively . . . walked out in a body.

walking out, walking our solid and intimate bodies down neighbouring streets lesbian-friendly or not, noting the houses other dykes enter, the rooms of artists one stripe or another. taking note of averted faces, elderly shoppers, ferocious dealers and those strung-out. or those who nod and smile hello. walking our passing bodies down streets of layered lives, lapidary, set in cement. the remains of stories.

touching the tree
touching the fence
alley alley home . . .

or moments like that warm expanse of shallow ocean
coming in, body of water rippling sandflat history in
names (Malaspina, Narváez). cool up to our knees, the
dog cavorting free of heat stupor (*Sutil, Mexicana,* and
Discovery). fur sprinkles glisten. late light's almost amber,
super-natural, islands to the west mere silhouettes
(Valdéz, Galiano, all that's left of their encounter with
Vancouver some two centuries ago and just offshore – the
same and not the same river-ocean then).

we cavort, wade, turn to go – and there, hallucinatory,
banked in ahistorical distance, a vertical construct of glass
and concrete flares its dazzle, flashes *"world-class city,"* the
city Vancouver *did not know that there would one day be.* . . .

allay home fears.

Your Perfect Home for sale. Open House cars arriving and leaving. Sunday drives with the Classifieds. "horrid little kitchen." "appalling colour scheme."

as if home –

shall I make some tea? he stands in the doorway, useless hands at his sides, unused to asking (long days ahead). in the sudden lapse when no one answers, Margo asks, shouldn't we notify someone?

bodies asleep on church steps, in doorways, under overpasses. bodies at sea in the streets of this city of reconstruction. unhoused: unnamed. collapse of social bedrock underneath.

it's the white truck lineup gives it away, that and the police cordon. in the crowd on the corner, dog and i watching, the old guy next to us confides, they did it in a day, you know. my room's up there (above the hardware store we're standing beside). i get up this morning and look out the window and wow, there's the American flag flying. it gave me a jolt i tell you, the Stars and Stripes over Hastings Street.

over a pristine *COUNTY COURTHOUSE*. moulded cornice, colonial shutters, porch with two white columns, classic pediment framing the door.

prefab, he says, they put it up in no time – just to blow it up, you wait and see.

Deeper down was something cool and fresh – endless garden.

but *whose* "Footprint"? you ask, staring down at a mosaic circle that features two splashes of koi colour, underwater gesture at the history of Dupont Street, erased and renamed Pender, this at Keefer and Gore. the footprint of many anonymous feet.

high as a kite. it was the flick of the sprockets as the end
flapped free. it was the smell of heated metal and over-
heated celluloid, his rare *damn it!*

just the smell drove us wild. those faded faces caught in a
blitz of light, smiles we recognized less and less burning up
in the mechanism of time. hands loose by their sides (touch
we'd known), facing the camera, voices we could no longer
conjure. sudden whirr and the loose end flapped free.

in the dazzle of empty screen as he called for the lights we
tumbled hysterical to the floor, trapped in the rewind of nos-
talgia here had erased. *what on earth is wrong with you three?*

not wild but low. No Spirits Here. *Ladies and Escorts*, ah, the
blues. the dumps, the mopes, the megrims. (grim me's).
flattened to a word, walls collapse with enough internal
pressure to blow the roof sky-high.

tea in hand, dog curled between us, cat on your lap. the inti-
mate comforts of home, its halo of pathways radiating out –

so?

so our neighbourhood bakery triumphs over the bar hands down. are we faded dykes?

i don't feel faded. and we're certainly not jaded.

hands reach for each other, knobby touch we know so well. reach for that space where our separate hours bump up against each other, mingle and melt. these bodies have an indeterminate while ahead, nowhere near as long as the years unravelling behind us.

so, *to put home into action.*

and if it's not just practice? my tongue exploring that delicious area of your hairline where your thoughts emerge, soft earlobe wordless, silent history of breast. and down, down the sensitive midline of you, cloud-flesh of belly, non-blue heaven without a single thought (will a kiss do? to keep you here?), nothing in the balance.

no one mentions the morgue (lugubrious word). no one
calls a funeral parlour. no one knows which one to call. call
her doctor, Dad advises. it seems a little late for that. his
thinning hair's a mess, he's been raking his hands through
it, back and forth, back and forth. we're still standing in the
doorway. none of us sit in the lounge.

mushroom, she insisted. sure of her colours. had they
changed in the last twenty years? dwindling visits from
overseas friends, people with plummy accents who
admired *the scenery* and smiled at our Canadian slang.

what lasted through the strain of time and distance? the
broken arcs? they declared they were *just the same* as they
sat reminiscing over drinks, ladies with their knees
together, feet tucked neatly below tweed skirts. men with
gallant manners, ready to laugh.

permutations of home. permeations from elsewhere. permanent quest.

on the radio now, the final bars of Chapman's "Grouse Mountain Lullaby" – solemn, funereal. what ever happened to *that jolly chairlift*?

hours passed, waiting for the doctor to arrive. we perched on her bed as if she might wake up and ask for her book, her glasses. unspoken questions filtering like dust. how? why? why now? we went on sitting in the hush as if one of us might hear the answer.

first home the maternal body the first one home re-enters. walks in through the door to its embrace. familiar palimpsest of smells. drip drip in the sink. pell-mell headlong rush of the dog down the stairs.

on our way to the Portuguese bakery we step around *Community in Bloom*, its rain-slick surface of ceramic bits embedded in the sidewalk, familiar frame of black triangles on white (shades of a compass rose pointing back, back in time). this one points to the block around it, renovated row-housing once inhabited by labourers and odd-jobbers, those new to the city, shiplap siding now brightly painted, image replete with cherry blossom, non-depicted gay gardeners, and, west instead of actual north, forever snowpeaks sheltering small roofs. *Community*, it says, through time translating

the home front.

1958

| *act two* |

... *that children being now come to the years of discretion, and having learned what their Godfathers and Godmothers prom-ised for them.* . . . . the cord so long attached, beginning to loosen, tightens in the moment of that phrase (who is Margo's Godmother? i wonder, which overseas friend?). i'm watching Margo's small back seated in the pew ahead, her short white veil one in a cloud of veils, a line of girls offering themselves up to the mystery of God. seated between my parents, my mother in her smartly tailored black coat, me in my new shortie, both of us wearing hats with little veils, i watch Mom place her gloved hand on

Lucy's knee to still her foot kicking the prayer-bench in front. Lucy in child-white socks and shoes. *Let thy fatherly hand, we beseech thee, ever be over them* . . . now it's Margo's turn to kneel before the Bishop for the laying on of hands. i'm trying to remember what i felt when it was my turn – something? anything? Father Worthy announces the final hymn and i stand in my new black pumps, almost as tall now as Dad, who gallantly extends his open hymn book to me.

Dearest Mother – Say a prayer that the house we saw will soon be ours! It is much the best we've seen – such a gorgeous view of the harbour and the city! Large enough for each of the girls to have her own room – and it is at the end of the road with woods behind the garden. No close neighbours, no more living in one another's pockets! We met the owner who lives in a rather grand Tudor-style house and seemed impressed with Charles' new position. It all seems too good to come true!

BC'ING YOU IN '58! Centennial Sam: red whiskers, battered felt hat and bandana riding his mule up the path of a century into the rising sun of *1958*.

C'mon pardner –
let's enjoy
the party!

*hot water radiators in every room! – no more buckets of sawdust
to lug. even empty it's beautiful and now it's ours. strange, those
rainbow wisps moving across the wall? – oh it's the cut-glass
doorknob catching the light. this hideous carpet has to go. why
on earth would anyone put beige with grey-blue walls? Charles
won't like the expense but a very light rose would look so much
better. I know we're going to be happy here – that's what rain-
bows mean.*

old bed, new satin eiderdown, new Hilroy scribbler. farm
girl kneeling on its cover looks like Donna – big smile as
she feeds a calf from a bucket.

*Tuesday. My room is so high up I can see the lights sparkling
across the water. Margo says it's nice but it's not home – she's
right. Mom loves her new wall-to-wall but we have to come in
through the basement and take off our shoes before we can come
upstairs. I don't think our friends will like it.*

**Tour the hustling, bustling . . . marvel at the industrial . . .
Pacific gateway to all corners of the world!**

here's to blue, luminous and clear after hours of gloom-
pounding rain and foggy windows on every soaked bus.
mountains appear while the city, expansive as ever, basks
in sun and money. brief November reprieve from flood-
ing drains, car backspray like boats' dousing unwary
pedestrians, steady dripline of awnings above umbrella
jostle. Chinatown quick with calls surfacing crimson and
gold. taking a shine to here, at home in the city's promise
we'd almost forgotten.

what about a goat? she said, wouldn't it be lovely, dear? we
could tether it in the vacant lot and then you could forget
about all those stones and weeds – goat's milk would be so
healthy for the girls.

and who would milk it? he asked.

THESE HANDS LEARNED BEAUTY
6 minutes of daily care for 6 weeks did this

Friday. I'm changing my name. Donna says Grade 10 is a good time to change. she says Suzie's got more pizzazz & it has, even if I'm still boring old Annie at home. Mom is never going to change – besides, I'm Suzanne whenever she's mad at me.

If there weren't enough grubby-looking characters here-abouts, the Centennial beard-growing bit is adding more victims by the hour.

all this hullabaloo about pioneers, she says, stirring the porridge. just an excuse to look scruffy if you ask me. what is so wonderful about plaid shirts and suspenders? and as for the women standing around wood stoves with their aprons on – well, nothing's changed very much, has it?

war paint she called it, getting ready to face a world of ladder climbing, gossip eyes at the office party. liquid foundation smoothed on, rouge applied and then removed in a critical second-thought's wipe-off. the silver lid lifted from her crystal powder bowl, its puff dipped, shaken and dipped again, not stroked but gentled onto cheeks, nose, forehead – a shine, she said, will spoil the effect. touch of eye shadow, mascara brush and the quick removal of clots. careful outline of lips and then the filling in of crimson, blotted on Kleenex. fluffing of hair. dab of Chanel behind each ear, the judicious choice of earrings, clipping each with a sideways glance to see how it looked. feet slipped into heels, chiffon scarf with its scent floating around her shoulders. finally the coat, dark, its lustrous fur, her neatly gloved hands turning up the collar to frame her face as Dad bends to bestow a kiss. *careful!* she warns. *you look lovely, my pet.* setting his hat on his head with a debonair tilt, he opens the stage door to the city for her.

on Sundays *Our Lord's Mother remains the type of highest womanhood.*

Saturday. Went skating with Bill + Bruce + D. She likes Bill a lot. She has dropped Bruce & is going to make a definite campaign for Bill. Bruce is okay, she says, but he's nothing special. I had to skate a lot with Bruce.

kept her countenance: put a good face on things.

The Odeon is showing *The Ten Commandments* with Charlton Heston. shall we take the girls to see it, Charles? so much more edifying than *Francis the Talking Mule.*

taking stock of the firsts that lagged behind Donna's alloweds: bra, lipstick (pink only), stockings and garter belt, shaving legs (*what nonsense! use the pumice stone*), high heels (pumps, not very high).

Misterioso, altero, *Violetta's repeating his words, such a gorgeous voice. Croce e delizia, the cross and delight of her heart – yes, both, both. such infuriating things, these boxer shorts – iron one crease and three more appear. Signor dell'avvenire – Seigneur, isn't that what the French call God? to think I'd never known what men wore before I married. but then, how would I? Mother called them "unmentionables" and of course the Boy handled all that – servant's work. I don't suppose Violetta ever ironed Alfredo's shorts.*

Rank after rank of towering concrete piers march across Second Narrows as construction goes ahead on 3,160-foot bridge.

my poppet, he called her, ruffling her hair.

all those adverts and not a thing worth looking at for $1.49! of course you have to pay for quality. now that jumper was a bargain, so were Lucy's shoes. and then the frilly blouse for Margo – a good buy. oh dear, at this rate we won't be home before your father. how long do frozen fish and chips take in the oven? hell's bells, this traffic is the limit – at least we've reached the bridge. oh, Annie, just look at that sunset! *well!* that chap in the car beside us just winked. what cheek! did he think I was looking at *him*? what does he think I am? with three children in the car too!

. . . a single, nuclear missile potent enough to wipe out Vancouver.

so what exactly *are* Communists? it's quiet and cool in the basement where the shoe bench is. Dad's hand is rubbing the brown leather of Mom's walking shoe with quiet care. Communists don't believe in private property, he says, they think the government should control everything. but why? well, they talk about equality but in fact people have to dance to the government's tune.

**Highways Minister Gaglardi . . . opened his new $150,000
Calvary Temple here on Sunday. . . . "Kamloops is for
Christ," he said. "Just watch our dust."**

can you believe it? Fiona tells me Dr. G. won't let his wife
wear makeup. and there he is, seeing women and their
private parts all day. doctors and priests, they're all the same.

we're strolling our fifteen-year-old bodies up the sidewalk in
halter tops and shorts, swinging our bags in rhythm, still
with the glow of Mahon Pool on our skin. Donna, who has
the curves, is walking closest to the traffic. a souped-up sedan
cruises along beside us, hands bang the car door, whistles,
yells. hey, doll! wanna ride, babe? ignore them, she says (her
walk slows, her eyelashes flutter), they're just hoods.

You were mad about the Coronation, devoured every scrap
of news you could get your hands on, pasted it all into that
big scrapbook. Now you pooh-pooh the parade for Princess
Margaret. What's happened to you?

Tuesday. At Donna's after school I talked to Wade. He is very good-looking even if his legs are paralyzed. Nobody talks about it in their family but I know it's from a car accident the night of his Grad party – everyone was drunk, guess he was too. Donna says he's awfully moody, but I think he's rather nice, in a dark sort of way. I wonder how much older he is.

looks don't count, not really. it's not about good looks, you know.

Saturday's the day for household jobs. clean up your room. help Dad burn rubbish in the incinerator. we're watching smoke and paper flakes spiral up to the firs. he's looking comfortable in his shabby gardening clothes and old hat, whacking down the bigger flakes with a stick. i'm feeding doodles and rough drafts to the flames. that was a good one, he says, the one you did on Pauline Johnson. standing there in his cast-off shirt hanging over my jeans i know i love him.

beautiful dust, *that's what Moses called her. Nefretiri, the Royal Princess. just* beautiful dust through which God works his purpose. *dust I suppose to <u>him</u>, once he'd turned his back on her. Charles thinks I've got it all wrong – of course he would! well, the parting of the Red Sea was a grand scene and at least the whole thing gave the girls a bit of history.*

i look a moron!
what about me? i look a kook!

we're peering at the black-and-white strip in our hands, three frames that were meant to retain our beauty-queen looks. velvet curtains of the photo booth hiding us as we struck poses for the mirror that flashed its Hollywood eye and betrayed us.

savagely scrawling *Donna the Moron* and *Suzie the Kook* we autographed our faces.

THE PERFECT SUBURBAN HOME

and its link

THE SECOND-LARGEST CANTILEVER SPAN IN CANADA

looking up as we drove past on the old bridge, we imagined we could see Donna's father behind the flare of a blowtorch on one of the girders vaulting their giant-legged way across the Narrows.

behind closed doors, a flare of voices from the dining room. dreaded end-of-the-month accounting for household expenses and she isn't good at it. she's sitting at the table with him, adding up her fistful of bills.

for Heaven's sake, Charles, I'm only a few cents out. what difference will a few cents make?

look, the cheque book has to balance. it's as simple as that.

oh! so you think I'm simple, do you!

(her slammed exit. one way out.)

robin rock rockin' at the sock hop as wallflowers watch, nodding in time, trying to look unrejected on the sidelines.

Dear Dorothy – Your visit bucked me up tremendously. How good it felt to laugh about the old days and all those awful mah-jong parties – Isn't it remarkable how we can pick up the threads after all this time? Before you arrived I was beginning to think I was getting peculiar – people here just don't seem to have a sense of humour.

Whipping up a Miracle
for women who think food should be fun

just the swans, a pink one and a black one keeping each other company in a trail of water lilies across the wall. transfers Donna's mom must have stuck up to brighten their bathroom full of tossed towels, toothbrushes and curlers, the apparatus Wade has to use, the little kids' plastic ducks. i stare at the swans' ruffled wings, how they're folded like hands in prayer as they sail serene,

serene across the tile while her dad rages on in Donna's
bedroom.

you think it's *funny* you get such a lousy grade? you think I
work at a high-risk job so you can fool around? look at your
brother, he may be a crip, but he's got a brain.

Blue, blue was the heaven above me . . .

not til you're sixteen, and that's final.

(*Sweet Little* . . . oh yeah.) but Mom, i am, almost. and every-
one else is dating *before* sixteen.

just thank your lucky stars we didn't pack you off to school
in England long ago. that's what we should have done. then
you'd have met a better class – not these hooligans with
greasy hair lounging about on Lonsdale whistling at girls.
what on earth is appealing about that?

oh boy!

Tuesday. D. gets all the babysitting jobs. Plus she's got the longest eyelashes of anyone. When we 2 are talking to boys they never take their eyes off her & I end up making catty remarks. Now she's flirting with M. even though she knows I like him. She's doing it just to show Brad who she caught smiling at Cindy. But M. doesn't know that so he lays on the charm. I don't see why she dropped Bill anyway.

what lucky stars?

what will he say this time, that wretched man? more fillings, more pain. and with a name like Silver! he's making pots of it off us at any rate. we're the ones paying for all that fancy equipment, patients at his mercy, sitting there with our mouths wide open like stupid sheep. I know what he's thinking behind his glasses – a slip of the drill, a bigger filling, make her pay for her rotten teeth!

essay on democracy. life cycle of the Douglas fir. conjugate
the verb *aimer*, present tense.

*Sunday. I'm such a birdbrain! Had a long talk with D. after
church. Brad's dating Cindy so Lynn, her sidekick, phoned D.
to tell her to lay off him. Poor D! She didn't say she wouldn't flirt
with M. but I don't think she will – she's a true friend.*

*Dearest Mother – First it was crinolines that had to be starched.
Then what they call pencil-line skirts, so tight a girl could barely
walk properly. Now the latest thing is a chemise. It balloons out
well below the waist with a little bow behind, and this in a full-
length winter coat! Rather uncomfortable I should think for
sitting in Church on a hard pew!*

up the mountain in light snow looking for specimens of
thuja, tsuga, taxus for Bi. laughing as it grows dark and
wandering flakes begin to fur our lashes – *I hear the call of
the singing firs* – Donna batting her snow-furred ones at me,
my tongue tripping out to lick them off. what time is it?

who cares! wild, wanting to fling us down in not-enough snow, wanting to fly through the woods in the secret light of our laughter. too late already to peel potatoes, we're in our mothers' bad books.

Dad announces over dinner, I think it's time we took out Canadian citizenship. Mom's scandalized. what? and give up our British passports? we wouldn't have to give them up, he explains. we could have dual citizenship. it would make more sense for the girls, don't you think? oh yes, Margo and i say as one. we know what the other is thinking: now we won't have to pretend when everyone sings *O Canada*.

keeping the account straight. no accounting for taste.

Thursday. D's house for supper, her Dad bragging about the guys he works with on the bridge, how tough they are. Wade must feel awful, why does he do it? There I was sitting between his big brawny arms reaching for the ketchup & W. gone all quiet in his wheelchair. He probably thinks I'm just a useless girl – too slow getting up to help with the dishes. Her mom teases me about sounding AWEfully polite, make yourself at home, she says. Oh sure, when her dad is going to pounce on D. for any little thing she says?

fever in the chestnut leaves unfurling, fever green and tender underfoot. hot rods parked in the school lot, hot noon shiny on chrome, fins, side-flames. Randy, butt in the palm of his hand, Brad with a bruise from the night before – pros bragging about wheelies and stack-ups, knuckle sandwiches, drag races past the Tomahawk, nights in the passion pit. and the broads with tight skirts and smart comebacks, broads who smack gum and bum smokes. even Donna's smoking, a little self-consciously. it's Wade, she says, just now and then, to keep him company you know. familiar smell of potato chips and Coke, hot gravel underfoot, a beat that's blasting through Brad's open car door –

sudden hands grab hands, doesn't matter whose, scores of sneakers, desert boots, black motorcycle boots, suede flatties stomp – who started this? – odd foolish grin, . . . *ain't nothin' but a*, what're we doing? who knows, just do it, *houn' daawg*, that lowdown grind-your-hips growl. past one, the buzzer's gone and nobody's breaking the circle. Mr. Kelly appears, just what is going on here? stomping up the worms, sir, someone shouts, yeah, worm stomp! worm stomp! along

with a few teachers he folds his arms and watches. they
have nothing to say above the noise of our feet pounding,
arms locked, legs like pistons smashing a hole in the sched-
ule, stomping up the words for something else –

*the city rubbed out. only dripping trees for company. if I
leave the ironing and walk to the other side of the house, the
bridge will be gone, and the rest of the world with it. does anyone
exist out there?*

**A hydrogen bomb dropped in the area would cause com-
plete destruction for a radius of 4 miles . . . You must get
beyond the 20 mile limit to be reasonably safe.**

what earthly use is that? she burst out at dinner. where
can people on the North Shore go? up that awful road
to Squamish until it peters out and then what? as for
the bridges – can you imagine the traffic? worse than
rush hour.

it's just a public safety notice, Dad said. there isn't going to
be a bomb.

couldn't you just die when he looks straight out at you!
we're glued to the screen, to the lock of dark hair swinging
above sad eyes as Elvis belts out "Heartbreak Hotel," his
sexy lips, his lopsided smile.

that sleazeball, Wade growls from his chair, he's got
nothing on Chuck Berry.

where's my lover-boy? Donna's mom slips into the room
behind Wade. she perches on the couch beside us, tucking
her feet up under her skirt. oh my, can he croon! some-
times she and Donna seem like sisters, only her mom's
face has more lines.

it's an insult, I tell you. those are still perfectly good suede
flatties – we bought them only a few months ago. how could
little shoes like that make too much noise? you must have
been dragging your feet in the school corridor. *tell your
mother you need new shoes*, indeed! they're trying to get at me,
that's what it is, trying to make me look a rotten mother!

holy smoke. for pete's sake. jeez.

*Friday. Why can't she be like D's mom, who's actually interested
in her life? I could've gone on a double date with D. tonight. She
wanted me to, she doesn't want to neck with Brad yet. If she gets
into trouble Mom will say I told you so – and it will all be her
fault. It's always I know what's best for you. I know No. That's
all she knows. Ina for short. Ina doesn't have a clue.*

I should have had sons. Daughters are such ungrateful
wretches. Sons adore their mothers. If I died tomorrow
would you even miss me? You'd miss your cook. You'd
miss your bloody char.

city lights and their romance, it's Gene Kelly singing in the
rain along the white line on Georgia and Granville only a
couple of blocks from the Medical-Dental. i could cross the
street, get lost in the crowd under all those lit-up mar-
quees, walk into the Vogue and catch *South Pacific* – Donna
would be so jealous! if i had the money. if Mom weren't

86

expecting me home to help with supper. if there weren't creepy old guys on the lookout for girls sitting alone.

rivers of doubt pouring through the house. tantrums over scissors not found, a lost sock, perceived insults. *hold your tongue and count to three.*

Dear Mother – Not much to report. The girls are doing well at school. With their sports this and clubs that they're hardly ever home. (I never thought it would be like this.) Charles is busy with the office and his volunteer work (evenings? what evenings together?). *The weather has been simply dreadful. I think I will repaint the bathroom.* (oh, what's the use?)

walking the road home from Donna's, beat of Wade's radio fading in my head . . . *Good Golly* and Holy Moly, late again. keeping it empty for whatever home weather will be when i step in the door. for now it's quiet, that quiet when think- ing stops and everything else comes forward – a whorl of light through trees at the churchyard corner. birds with rainbow backs, their flash of green to purple when they turn, preening their hearts out. birds don't have to think, they just sing out that swelling in their throats, that joysong on the instant, instantly being.

Doctors! They're all alike. Just like my father always passing judgment. What does Gravell know with his smarmy smile and fake sympathy? I don't need a psychiatrist. All I need is a pre-scription for something to help me sleep.

. . . some folks on a bus like to have a quiet peaceful moment to think. They would be grateful if you would switch your portable radios off.

<u>Saturday</u>. Dad's going to teach me to drive so I can run errands for Mom & drive Lucy and Margo to Guides when Mom is too tired. I just called D. to tell her we can go to all the neat places, up to Princess Pool, down to the Tomahawk. We won't need dates, we'll be free!

Dad's red roses don't seem to help a *Blue Lady*.

reading in the tree-shadowed cool of the den when the phone rings. Suzie? it's Donna. have you heard? – her voice sounds strange – it's really bad. the bridge just collapsed.

oh no! she isn't talking any more and i don't know what to say. there's a radio announcer's voice loud in their kitchen and Wade beginning to shout about her using the phone. where's your mom? she's gone down there. fear hums along the line between us. Wade yells some more and she says 'bye in a choked voice.

which bridge? oh *that* one. thank God it's not the one Charles comes home on.

ambulance sirens down the hill. the radio reports scores of rescue boats – crushed steel, crushed men – (i call Donna and Wade says they haven't heard anything yet) – doctors and nurses are volunteering, people calling in to give blood – switchboard at the hospital has no information – a crowd has gathered onshore, many with bowed heads – some ambulances are going to the General overtown – (i call again: Wade says they still haven't heard and Donna's putting the little ones to bed).

stop making a nuisance of yourself, Mom says, you're just tying up their phone line.

the first span, the one with the big overhang, came down . . . men hurtling toward water . . . as the first span settled in a cloud of spray, the second one began to fall . . .

the count: 16 men dead, 2 missing, 20 hospitalized.

not one wink of sleep, I tell you, with that wretched dog barking its head off all night long. what kind of people keep a dog chained up outside? are they deaf? are they dead? Charles, you'll have to call them again. they won't even speak to me.

Wednesday. *Donna's Dad is ALIVE!! Her mom found him last night in the General over town. He's alive but he's still unconscious.*

that spot is cursed. Fate had a hand in this, you mark my words. all those accidents with the old bridge over the years. and now eighteen men gone, probably more in the end. that poor woman. she'll be left with four children, well the oldest is hardly a child but what use can he be to her in a wheelchair?

bridling at her words, at the words so marked.
Donna, i'm keeping my fingers crossed for you.

all that vainglory, all that talk of triumphing over the Narrows. in the end it all comes tumbling down like dominoes. a broken W in the water. does nobody see it? W for will. that's what it means, collapsed will. as if I didn't know . . .

and there was Pauline's story shadowing the news about *black murky waters* where the diver drowned, looking for bodies. it was the salt-chuck oluk's stain. had Pauline fudged the Chief's ending? perhaps the Tenas Tyee hadn't really cleared that *trail of blackness.*

a rotten shame, he said. those lives lost and all that money down the drain. we taxpayers will have to foot the bill of course. no doubt some engineer is going to have to pay for this.

if only I could sleep. just a few hours. The Moving Finger writes – *so many words, so many words all night.* The Moving Finger writes – *and it's indelible. who next?*

<u>Friday</u>. *At D's all afternoon. Her mother goes to the hospital every day so she's being mom for the little kids. Their house was a mess. I helped her tidy up, W. in a rage the whole time. She says their neighbours have been bringing food over. Why don't we? I asked Mom. Suit yourself, she said. Doesn't she care?*

how can the sun be shining? Margo and Lucy batting the shuttlecock around on the grass and laughing. the world feels odd. there's the wrecked bridge in the harbour and Donna's dad gone and the whole world just carries on. there's sky and the close-up smell of grass growing – right through an empty space that none of us can see. is this what Donna's thinking?

I know they're around and I know they hate me, that's why they won't let me sleep. be reasonable, Charles says. it's just this gloom around the bridge, that's what it is. but they've always been around, I've always known they have, these evil ones, waiting for the right moment.

what's wrong with Mom?

i don't know.

Friday. I sat with Donna & her family in Church. Mom wouldn't go. She said Church couldn't change anything. Donna

& her mom cried a lot, Wade didn't. Where was God? The Bible
says not even the smallest sparrow falls without Him knowing.
So where was He when the bridge collapsed?

we're wading into the rushes at the far end of Princess
Pool, away from the smell of suntan oil and beer, away
from wisecracks and cannonball jumps from the dam.
Donna's quiet. the trees around us are quiet. what is she
thinking? i've found a job, she says, i start tomorrow.
where? at the Safeway on Lonsdale. a real job, i think.
cashier, she says, i'm good enough at math. but you're not
old enough. i told them i was sixteen. just for the summer?
maybe, she says. you can't leave school, i say, you just can't.

CENTENNIAL ACTIVITIES GEARING UP
North Van aims to celebrate

it's good practice for you. Dad sounds encouraging as we
drive onto the old Second Narrows Bridge, its metal deck-
work slippery in rain. just remember to keep the wheel

steady. my knuckles white against skidding. the wreck of the new bridge looms beside us. keep your eyes on the road, he snaps. this bad luck bridge, this bad luck crossing.

you're going to stall, he's tense beside me. give her more gas. i can't, we'll skid. gear down then. is the lift section going to rise? keep going, you have a green light.

we jerk along, my foot hovering between accelerator and brake, slow / fast / slow, towards the solid bulk of the grain elevators there on the other side.

Dear Mother . . . Dear Moth . . . er, we are all . . . (err) . . . well . . .

LATE IN THE DAY

| *finale* |

you forget – what is it you forget?

not deliberately. contours of memory-landscape, signifi-
cant features of its stories shift with the years, eroded by
changing weather systems. so home. so the more and
more homeless, now that it's late in the day. darkness sur-
rounds us with the heavy machinery of increasing rain. if
sleep calls, it's to shelter your face in the pillow of a brief
respite from the news.

i hear your familiar sounds in the bathroom getting ready for bed. the tap running – you brushing your teeth. long pause – you're reading something. there's the flush. soon you will pad into our darkened room, slide into your side of the bed, and i will turn over to greet your kiss, its gentle, persistent question.

we? at its farthest ebb.

in the still of almost evening, something to burn for those who have left, who go on burning in us. *tsa sur.* brimming bowls and incense. water and light.

it was July – no rain, no flooding streets. the brilliance of this city basking in blue infinity over our heads, mountains hunkered down in hot rock-slow time as if they knew nothing of shift. traffic streams. radio reaches. plush, all plush we think, until the body blinks, taking mountains, air, and traffic with it.

don't go without saying goodbye. it's not about Ps and Qs or even the simple social need to recognize connection. a hole in the day sudden departure leaves.

we were cleaning our brushes under the running tap when i asked why do you think they want to punish you? she worked at the bristles for a minute longer, working out specks of blue latex. because i'm still here. what do you mean? (what does *mean* mean?) just wait, she said, just be glad you don't know.

in the home country a daughter sings in her untried wisdom, wanting to know:

Things, a bird skimming across a window, were a sort of writing on a wall.

disaster fears. dis-astre.
up against the stars and their foregone orbits. conclusive.

. . . this heavy, leaden body . . . whatever became of the indefati-
gable, birdlike body that had been hers . . . ?

snow underfoot late in earth's day and unseasonably early.
mauve clouds dusking deeper over the rooflines sun has
dropped below. as we approach the end of the park, a
couple separates from behind a pine tree. he stoops to
chuck the dog's soft ear and strides off, leaving her to avoid
our eyes, fingers nervous at her tight jeans.

at the other end of the park, a massive snowball hulks,
alone at the bottom of its green path down a slope.
someone's stuck a twiggy branch on top and dangled a
silver pencil flashlight from it – Xmas mockery? a public
greeting with what's to hand?

if home represents what is dear to us . . .

such soft pink light is hard to read by. glancing away from
the tea she had just sipped, that amused half-mocking

smile with its embarrassed edge when she declared they were out to get her hid a dare under the flyaway hair, soft sag of cheek, the look that slid off truth, posing it there: can't you see what's under your nose?

home truth. *domestic; opp. to foreign*

the lay of the city, memory setting the distance straight if we can call it up at all under the lie of hoardings hiding cavern-holes in the ground mammoth equipment slopes down, (vacancy), dozers, dump trucks, crane erections towering – memory deconstructed so that we end up asking, well, what used to be here?

couldn't talk about her body in its presence. couldn't talk about the softness of her hair on the pillow, lashes stuck to her cheek, eyes dead asleep. couldn't talk about it wrapped in her private cocoon, so we stepped into the hall and stood between the doorways to their separate bedrooms.

should we call the morgue?

what morgue? where?

maybe we should call the police.

dying in your sleep isn't a crime.

but we don't know . . .

maybe we should call a funeral parlour.

he came out then from the kitchen. you'll have to call her doctor.

her doctor? what can a doctor do?

he has to sign the death certificate.

(public words at last to break it open.)

you are gradually speaking less and less of elsewhere. that sharp pang of the place you didn't want to leave is fading. the you i know stretches its recognition network into these streets, their ghosts and echoes. amazed at how the wintry ribbing of mammoth chestnut trees on the corner has canopied out from an early photograph where those same trees stood small by a picket fence outside the carefully carpentered house that Harris built and Zitko took over, turning what had been a stable into a bakery. house and bakery long since levelled, along with the rest of the block, to make a park to replace another park levelled and built into anonymous low-cost housing.

close up. as if a blanket and jacket sodden for nights now in the rain and left on a log between still-standing trees might hold the transient shape of one who took shelter there.

the mother sings in her silence: learn to read, my daughter, read the signs as you sit in the endless waiting room.

At the Woodwards' Squat I was able to find mattresses and tarps, which keep me dry and relatively comfortable for sleeping, as opposed to being in the parks or doorways.

in the mother country.

in the stillness after she's slammed the front door we stand in the void of the kitchen. the tea towel she's flung at Dad hangs limply from his hands. my hands are hot in the sudsy water. finally, i look at him.

she's having a breakdown, he says. you're going to have to help her more around the house.

i'm trying to, but she gets so angry all the time, or else she's sleeping. what's wrong with her?

the doctor says she's depressed.

because of us? i've turned off the tap and he's still standing there.

not because of you. finally he picks up a plate and starts to wipe. no one seems to know, he sighs. her doctor says it's quite common in women.

pre-ordained? fatal attraction? Coming, the billboard
said.

between this love and its body, clogged air, dirty water, oil-
rig fire. nothing uncompromised or clear.

hypocrites! they say one thing and they mean another –
always talking out of the other side of their mouths.

only a few leaves left on birches after the snow, wet and
unaccountably early, broke the stems by which they were
hanging on, luminous hands clapping in sudden high-
intensity winds.

I didn't marry a *house* for heaven's sake – though I might
just as well have. you're always running off to this or that.
and your father with his eternal evening work when it isn't

the Church calling. who am I supposed to keep the home fires burning for? just tell me that!

out of doors. walking in the fog of depression. unhoused people enclosed in the broke and broken halves of their day, unhinged. our common world unhinged with them.

round and round the square that is a park he trudges, a bristle of silence against smiling joggers, talkative morning constitutionalists, dogwalkers and tai chiers. hunched in shabby jacket against the cold, white beard streaming prophetic, plastic bag tucked under one arm, he paces an endless circuit around the almost empty cup of the earth. hey little buddy, he growls at the small white dog trotting past. neither dog nor man will appear in a sidewalk mosaic.

but why? no answer.
why now after all this time? still no answer.

two young mothers probing the air around their mother's body curled under a pink blanket pulled up to her chin. as if the hottie, as if the cup of steaming tea, as if the novel, that book of plot solutions from an earlier time, could materialize before them.

the body of this earth. tufted pine branch swirl multi-directional. crossed by the shadow of a wind-tossed crow.

while you, snug on the other end of the couch, cat on your lap, you dearly familiar, talk about what you feel on these streets occupied by despair a loonie here, a toonie there won't end. so many glass walls, each one a private hell, and people encased, trying to make some semblance of home on the street.

connections splay out between images, cross thought traffic, don't form throughways or one-way sense.

having stepped back into the steep of Red Rose, of cozy and pot, the everywhere smear of lemon polish, tea biscuit crumbs where once were scones, the fetid flower stink of empty vases' water-rings – edging up to piles of ironing we'd left behind, the nightly push of the mop across the kitchen floor, bleach cleanser smell of a scoured tub, all gloss gone – encountering still the curfew, the answering-to, the guilt of containment we'd struck out from and were meant to replicate. and do, at times. still do.

not just a housewife. not *a parasite* . . . *a sponger* . . . *a bum.*

a stifled bomb. deactivated.

it's all about waiting, my girl. that's what waiting rooms are for. you queue up to pay at this or that tollbooth. you line up at this or that Pearly Gate, waiting for your reward, which never comes.

so what were they writing, those birds, with their flour-
ishes hieroglyphic? their feathered liftoff into the eye's
vanishing point?

it must be hard, you say, for the Tibetan Buddhists who
escaped to India or Canada – their longing for Tibet, for
home, and at the same time knowing that the permanence
of home is an illusion.

if home represents what is dear to us, it costs the earth.

pell-mell to the mall, let's say, the blare of status signs,
brand-name blazons and select chainstore chic cast over
the benches of the exhausted middle-aged marooned with
their bags, where young pimps troll, and clock-driven
receptionists nurse stiletto feet before leaping up for their
next foray into allure.

bringing it all back home.

was she ready to go? did she know she was leaving, ready or not?

there was the already wrapped and tagged gift on her dresser, which, unwrapped, turned out to be a box of body powder for the daughter who never used body powder, whose birthday was still a week away. was this a sign?

more to the point, there was the empty glass of water under her bedside lamp, and beside it an empty bottle of sleeping pills.

it could have been almost empty, she might have taken the last one last night.

but it could have been full. she might have been saving them up.

then wouldn't she leave a note?

background *thunk thunk* of a piledriver somewhere on the waterfront. splashy and immediate the sound tires make rolling through a puddle down the alley. the tin can glassy sound of someone rifling through blue recycling boxes. routine sounds. splintered by a siren magnifying Hastings Street on its way to Main.

alley alley home . . .

blue light and the mixed blue of blues. dark under seemly or seemingly pure white. mountains rise up into the clear.

There will be a series of propane devices placed on the 1st and 2nd floor windows that will be set off to simulate an explosion during our filming on Thursday. There will be some noise, of course, and debris from the building will fall onto Heatley Street.

that sense of falling – running, running through the dream to get somewhere – where already nowhere real.

we were burglars, rifling through her things, half-expecting she would rise up newly awake and demand to know what on earth we thought we were doing. caught with our hands searching her dresser, caught red-handed searching for a note, a letter, a string of words to explain her body inert on the bed behind us.

they are too strong for me it said. that's all it said. a private scrap of paper.

home unravels backwards: to lie; bed, couch, night's lodging; to lie yet not to lie: beloved, dear.

he was sitting on the sofa in the living room, head in his hands, locked in wordlessness. i put my arm around his shoulders as he lifted red-rimmed eyes to mine. if only i hadn't waited so long. she said she was tired last night so i let her sleep. if only i hadn't. if i'd found her sooner . . .

how to say it gently enough? it wouldn't have made any difference, Dad.

unlocking the door of an unfamiliar empty house – that glimpse, soon to be erased, of how it holds its emptiness without us. not home yet. not that construction of habit we will place upon it. we camp in its strangeness for three days without belongings, note when sun arrives in each window, mystified by sounds and their directions. the house feels blind, you say, on its unwindowed sides. still not home, we perch on its front steps with borrowed cups of tea, watching the cat sniff each leaf.

expatriates, you note, from shadow homes, want to nest differently.

at the end of the next block, five mothers are dancing, five women hand-in-hand across the track a mammoth loco-motive is bearing down with its one-eyed light – stopped. the Militant Mothers of Raymur are standing their ground, triumphant letters brash around them, demanding an overpass to stop their kids' death-defying runs to school on the other side. they were, mothers and kids, already on the other side of the tracks: City Council turned deaf ears. so they stopped the trains to the waterfront dead in their tracks. the gist of their story a mosaic retrieves in small pieces from the emptiness underlying history.

sun switched on, the city glows in its unhallowed past, reflecting shallow pools of remembrance in plate glass towers, copper echoes, false fronts.

after the doctor has come and gone, certifying death due to a coronary – an autopsy would be too hard on your father. at least if she did, she made a good job of it. after the call to the funeral parlour, we sit beside her, watching brown stains appear on her skin. the longer we sit, the more her body seems to estrange itself – not-Mom, not any of the names we called her by.

not home. never at home in what remains. yet caught in the here of it.

i was on my way to the ATM, running through my mental list, when she stopped me at the corner of Main in a rush of light-driven shoppers, scabs on her face, birdsnest hair, but the arrested urgency in her eyes, and words so cracked they were barely audible over the traffic, *anything? even pennies?*

here, i said. i was always saying here.

sun cracked its way through curtains she had drawn against eventual day. her room seemed small, the pull of her body gone. i was desperate to get out. through the hall, through the kitchen, the half-open door to climb the first rockery step in that huge and unfamiliar light. roses star-tlingly neon, small tree – i recognized its shimmering. in it a single sparrow, head cocked eyeing me. i stop headlong as it opens its beak to pour out all that the room, her body, her house, could not. home-free.

NOTES AND SOURCES

I am indebted to all the books, articles, newspapers, and historic photographs that have jogged my memory and shaped my thinking for this book. Of the photographs, I owe particular gratitude to two exhibitions: "Fred Herzog: Vancouver Photographs," Vancouver Art Gallery 2007, and "Unfinished Business: Vancouver Street Photographs 1955 to 1985," Presentation House, North Vancouver, 2003.

Not all material that looks like a quote in *The Given* is a quote. Some fragments in italics are invented. The following are not:

First epigraph: Robin Blaser, "Author's Note," *The Holy Forest, Collected Poems of Robin Blaser*. The Regents of the University of California, University of California Press, Berkeley and Los Angeles, 2006. p. xxv.

Second epigraph: Pema Chödrön, "Weather and the Four Noble Truths," *Comfortable with Uncertainty*. Copyright ©

SEVEN GLASS BOWLS

Page 3. Ethel Wilson. "Tuesday and Wednesday" in *The Equations of Love*. Macmillan of Canada, Toronto, 1952. p. 48.

Page 5, bottom. Virginia Woolf. *Between the Acts*. Vintage Classics, Random House, London, 2000. p. 97.

Page 7. Marguerite Duras. *Duras by Duras*. City Lights Books, San Francisco, 1987. p. 16.

Page 9. Francesco Maria Piave. Libretto for Giuseppe Verdi's *La Traviata* (1851). Act 1, Violetta's aria "È strano!"

Page 9. Virginia Woolf. *Moments of Being*. A Harvest Book, Harcourt Brace & Company, San Diego, New York, London, 1985. p. 116.

Page 10. Marguerite Duras and Xavière Gauthier. *Woman to Woman* (trans. Katharine A. Jensen), University of Nebraska Press, Lincoln and London, 1987. p. 68. Reprinted by kind permission of the University of Nebraska Press.

Page 12. "Teddy Bears' Picnic." Music by John W. Bratton 1907, words by Jimmy Kennedy 1932.

Page 12. *The Shorter Oxford English Dictionary*. Guild Publishing, London, 1988. p. 976.

Page 14. Piave. *La Traviata*. Act 1.

Page 14. Duras & Gauthier. p. 69.

Pages 15, 17. Excerpted from *The Conversations at Curlow Creek* by David Malouf. Copyright © 1996 by David Malouf. Reprinted by permission of Knopf Canada. p. 39.

1953

Pages 25, 37. Viktor Léon and Leo Stein, Libretto for Franz Lehár's *The Merry Widow*, 1905. Act 11.

Page 29. Pauline Johnson. "The Two Sisters" in *Legends of Vancouver*. Saturday Sunset Presses, Vancouver, 1913, p. 1.

Page 30. *North Shore Review*, March 21, 1952.

Page 34. *The Province*, June 10, 1952.

Page 36. Sir Carleton Allen. "The Crown and the Commonwealth," *Coronation Number, Queen Elizabeth 11*, ed. Sir Bruce Ingram. The Illustrated London News and Sketch Ltd., London, 1953.

Page 37. *North Shore Review*, January 9, 1952.

Pages 41, 44. *The Province*, March 30, 1953.

Page 42. *The Vancouver Sun*, October 28, 1955.

Page 43. Diana Gray, Tillicum Editor. *The Province Tillicum Club*. March 1953.

Page 46. *North Shore Review*, June 2, 1952.

Page 48. Dorothy Richardson. "Honeycomb," *Pilgrimage* 1. Reprinted by permission of Paterson Marsh Ltd. on behalf of the Estate of Dorothy Richardson. University of Illinois Press reprint, Urbana and Chicago, 1979. p. 424.

Pages 49, 54. *Old Vancouver Townsite Walking Tour*. Footprints Community Art Project, Vancouver, 2003. p. 38.

Page 49. Richardson, "Honeycomb." p. 425.

Page 50. Joe Francis. "Skid Row," *A Hurricane in the Basement*. Portrait V2K: The City of Vancouver Millennium Project, Vancouver, 2000. p. 54.

Page 51. Excerpted from *The Beauty Myth* by Naomi Wolf. Copyright © 1990 by Naomi Wolf. Reprinted by permission of Random House of Canada. p. 70.

Page 53. Joe Francis, p. 54.

Page 56. George Bowering. *Bowering's B.C.: A Swashbuckling History*. Viking, Penguin Books Canada, Toronto, 1996. p. 58.

Page 58. Richardson, p. 425.

1958

Pages 65, 66. "The Order of Confirmation," *The Book of Common Prayer*. Society for Promoting Christian Knowledge, The University Press, Cambridge, n.d., pp. 297, 299.

Pages 66, 67. B.C. Centennial poster reproduced in *Vancouver's First Century: A City Album 1860–1960*,

eds. Anne Kloppenborg, Alice Niwinski,
Eve Johnson, Robert Gruetter. J.J. Douglas,
Vancouver, 1977. p. 151.

Page 68. *North Shore Press-Review*, January 9, 1958.

Page 69. *Good Housekeeping* ad for handcream,
February 1958.

Page 69. *North Shore Press-Review*, January 23, 1958.

Pages 70, 71. *North Shore Press-Review*, January 2, 1958.

Page 71. Herbert F. Tomkinson. *My Prayer Book: For
Women and Girls*. Longmans, Green & Co.,
New York and Toronto, 1957. p. 58.

Page 72. Piave. *La Traviata*. Act 1.

Page 72. *The Province*, November 27, 1956.

Page 73. *The Province*, January 14, 1958.

Page 74. *The Province*, January 6, 1958.

Pages 76, 77. *The Sun*, January 2, 1958.

Page 78. *Good Housekeeping* ad for mayonnaise,
February 1958.

Page 79. Archibald Lampman. "Life and Nature,"
The Penguin Book of Canadian Verse, ed. Ralph
Gustafson. Penguin Books, Hammondsworth,
1958. p. 70.

Page 81. Pauline Johnson. "The Lost Lagoon," *Canadian
Poets*, ed. John William Garvin, 1916. p. 152.

Page 83. Worm Stomp rendition of Elvis Presley singing
"Hound Dog," 1956.

Page 84. *Civil Defense Evacuation and Survival Plan for
Greater Vancouver Target Area*, 1957. Quoted in *Vancou-
ver's First Century*. p. 151.

Page 88. "Don't Rock Buses," *The Buzzer*, October 17, 1958. Quoted in *Vancouver's First Century*. p. 143.

Page 90. Eyewitness account of Les Wells, in *The Province*, June 18, 1958.

Page 92. Pauline Johnson. "The Sea-Serpent," *Legends of Vancouver*. p. 57.

Page 92. Omar Khayyám. *The Rubáiyát of Omar Khayyám*, trans. Edward Fitzgerald, 1859, stanza 51.

LATE IN THE DAY

Page 99. H.D. *HERmione*. New Directions, New York, 1981. p. 125.

Page 100. Marguerite Duras. *The Ravishing of Lol Stein*, trans. Richard Seaver. First Evergreen Black Cat, Grove Press, New York, 1968. p. 44.

Page 103. "Frank" from "26 Affidavits in Defense of the Woodwards Squat." Woodwards Squat website, 2002.

Page 108. Helen Gurley Brown, *Sex and the Single Girl*. Cited in Barbara Ehrenreich and Deirdre English. *For Her Own Good*. Anchor Books, Doubleday, New York, 1989, p. 288.

Page 111. Corruptor Productions Services Notice of Filming, 2001.

ACKNOWLEDGEMENTS

An earlier version of "Seven Glass Bowls" appeared as a chapbook, *Seven Glass Bowls*, from Nomados Press, Vancouver, 2003 – my thanks to Peter and Meredith Quartermain. An earlier version of "Out of the Blue" appeared in the *Capilano Review* – my thanks to Sharon Thesen. An excerpt from "1958" appeared in *Prairie Fire* – my thanks to Andris Taskans. An excerpt from "Late in the Day" appeared in *Rampike* – my thanks to Karl Jirgens.

Warm thanks to my editor, Stan Dragland, for his very patient and expert eye, and to Ellen Seligman, Anita Chong, and Jenny Bradshaw at M&S, for their care with the details of this manuscript.

My gratitude to all those friends and family who have discussed and encouraged the writing of this book over the years, especially to my sister, Pam Pedersen, who shared her memories, and Leila Sujir, Lydia Kwa, Meredith Quartermain, Jane Munro, Lorri Neilson, and Kathy Mezei, with special thanks to Liz Hay and George Bowering. My deepest thanks to Bridget Mackenzie, for, without her unfailing faith in this project, it would never have been finished. Particular thanks to Rick Rova for ever-patient technical help. And, as always, my gratitude to Zasep Tulku Rinpoche for his remarkable teachings.

Thanks to Robert Majzels, Aritha Van Herk, Louise Forsyth, and students of the creative writing program at the University of Calgary, who sat through a long afternoon of hearing the full manuscript in January 2007.

I am grateful for the periods of sustained writing time that 1997 and 2004 Canada Council Writing Grants and a B.C. Arts Council Grant in 2001 have given me.